INTERROGATIONS AT NOON

INTERROGATIONS AT NOON

• • •

POEMS BY

Dana Gioia

Graywolf Press
SAINT PAUL, MINNESOTA

Publication of this volume is made possible in part by a grant
provided by the Minnesota State Arts Board through an appropriation
by the Minnesota State Legislature, and by a grant from the National
Endowment for the Arts. Significant support has also been provided by
the Bush Foundation; Dayton's Project Imagine with support from
Target Foundation; the McKnight Foundation; a grant made on
behalf of the Stargazer Foundation; and other generous
contributions from foundations, corporations, and individuals.
To these organizations and individuals we offer our heartfelt thanks.

Published by Graywolf Press
2402 University Avenue, Suite 203
Saint Paul, MN 55114
All rights reserved.

www.graywolfpress.org

Published in the United States of America

ISBN: 1-55597-318-3

4   6   8   9   7   5

Library of Congress Catalog Number: 00-105071

Cover art: Christopher Pekoc, *Interrogations at Noon*

Cover design: Jeanne Lee

ACKNOWLEDGMENTS

These poems, often in significantly different versions, have previously appeared in the following journals: *Acumen, Chronicles, Connecticut Review, The Dark Horse, Eckerd College Review, Eclectic Literary Review, The Formalist, Image, Light Quarterly, New Criterion, Northeast Corridor, Oxford Poetry, The Philadelphia Inquirer, Poetry, River Styx, San Francisco Magazine, Sequoia, The Southern Review, Verse,* and *Wigwag.*

"The Voyeur," "Failure," "The Litany," "Metamorphosis," "My Dead Lover," "Unsaid," "For Sale," "Elegy with Surrealist Proverbs as Refrain," "Accomplice," "A California Requiem," "Words," "The Bargain," "The End of the World," and "The Lost Garden" first appeared in the *Hudson Review.* Two of the translations of Valerio Magrelli, "I have often imagined" and "I have from you," first appeared in *Poetry.* "The Litany" was reprinted in *The Best American Poetry 1997.*

"Interrogations at Noon" was commissioned by the British Broadcasting Corporation for National Poetry Day, 1999.

"Juno Plots Her Revenge" and "The Litany" were each published as chapbooks by Aralia Press. "Long Distance," "Alley Cat Serenade," and "Curriculum Vitae" were published as Aralia Press broadsides. Thirteen poems also appeared in an Aralia Press limited edition, *The Lost Garden.*

Eleven of these poems were printed in a bilingual limited edition, *Unsaid / Non Detto,* published in Verona, Italy, by La Chimerea Officina.

The author wishes to thank all of these editors and printers for their generosity and support.

For Mary

As not the world can praise too much

—BEN JONSON

CONTENTS

I.

II.

III. Words for Music

· I ·

Human speech is like a cracked kettle on which we beat crude rhythms for bears to dance to, while we long to make music that will melt the stars.

—GUSTAVE FLAUBERT

WORDS

The world does not need words. It articulates itself
in sunlight, leaves, and shadows. The stones on the path
are no less real for lying uncatalogued and uncounted.
The fluent leaves speak only the dialect of pure being.
The kiss is still fully itself though no words were spoken.

And one word transforms it into something less or other—
illicit, chaste, perfunctory, conjugal, covert.
Even calling it a *kiss* betrays the fluster of hands
glancing the skin or gripping a shoulder, the slow
arching of neck or knee, the silent touching of tongues.

Yet the stones remain less real to those who cannot
name them, or read the mute syllables graven in silica.
To see a red stone is less than seeing it as jasper—
metamorphic quartz, cousin to the flint the Kiowa
carved as arrowheads. To name is to know and remember.

The sunlight needs no praise piercing the rainclouds,
painting the rocks and leaves with light, then dissolving
each lucent droplet back into the clouds that engendered it.
The daylight needs no praise, and so we praise it always—
greater than ourselves and all the airy words we summon.

THE VOYEUR

. . . and watching her undress across the room,
oblivious of him, watching as her slip
falls soundlessly and disappears in shadow,
and the dim lamplight makes her curving frame
seem momentarily both luminous
and insubstantial—like the shadow of a cloud
drifting across a hillside far away.

Watching her turn away, this slender ghost,
this silhouette of mystery, his wife,
walk naked to her bath, the room around her
so long familiar that it is, like him,
invisible to her, he sees himself
suspended in the branches by the window,
entering this strange bedroom with his eyes.

Seen from the darkness, even the walls glow—
a golden woman lights the amber air.
He looks and aches not only for her touch
but for the secret that her presence brings.
She is the moonlight, sovereign and detached.
He is a shadow flattened on the pavement,
the one whom locks and windows keep away.

But what he watches here is his own life.
He is the missing man, the loyal husband,
sitting in the room he craves to enter,
surrounded by the flesh and furniture of home.
He notices a cat curled on the bed.
He hears a woman singing in the shower.
The branches shake their dry leaves like alarms.

INTERROGATIONS AT NOON

Just before noon I often hear a voice,
Cool and insistent, whispering in my head.
It is the better man I might have been,
Who chronicles the life I've never led.

He cannot understand what grim mistake
Granted me life but left him still unborn.
He views his wayward brother with regret
And hardly bothers to disguise his scorn.

"Who is the person you pretend to be?"
He asks, "The failed saint, the simpering bore,
The pale connoisseur of spent desire,
The half-hearted hermit eyeing the door?

"You cultivate confusion like a rose
In watery lies too weak to be untrue,
And play the minor figures in the pageant,
Extravagant and empty, that is you."

FAILURE

As with any child, you find your own more beautiful —
eager to nurse it along, watch over it,
and taking special pride as each day
it grows more gorgeously like you.

Why not consider it a sort of accomplishment?
Failure doesn't happen by itself. It takes time,
effort, and a certain undeniable gift.
Satisfaction comes from recognizing what you do best.

Most of what happens is never intended,
but deep inside you know you planned this —
not a slip or a fumble but a total rout.
You only fail at what you really aim for.

DIVINATION

Always be ready for the unexpected.
Someone you have dreamed about may visit.
Better clean house to make the right impression.
There are some things you should not think about.

Someone you have dreamed about may visit.
Is it an old friend you do not recognize?
There are some things you should not think about.
Who is the stranger standing at the door?

Is it an old friend you do not recognize?
Notice the cool appraisal of his eyes.
Who is the stranger standing at the door?
You sometimes wonder what you're waiting for.

Notice the cool appraisal of his eyes.
Better clean house to make the right impression.
You sometimes wonder what you're waiting for.
Always be ready for the unexpected.

ELEGY WITH SURREALIST PROVERBS
AS REFRAIN

"Poetry must lead somewhere," declared Breton.
He carried a rose inside his coat each day
to give a beautiful stranger—"Better to die of love
than love without regret." And those who loved him
soon learned regret. "The simplest surreal act
is running through the street with a revolver
firing at random." Old and famous, he seemed *démodé*.
There is always a skeleton on the buffet.

Wounded Apollinaire wore a small steel plate
inserted in his skull. "I so loved art," he smiled,
"I joined the artillery." His friends were asked to wait
while his widow laid a crucifix across his chest.
Picasso hated death. The funeral left him so distressed
he painted a self-portrait. "It's always other people,"
remarked Duchamp, "who do the dying."
I came. I sat down. I went away.

Dali dreamed of Hitler as a white-skinned girl—
impossibly pale, luminous and lifeless as the moon.
Wealthy Roussel taught his poodle to smoke a pipe.
"When I write, I am surrounded by radiance.
My glory is like a great bomb waiting to explode."
When his valet refused to slash his wrists,
the bankrupt writer took an overdose of pills.
There is always a skeleton on the buffet.

Breton considered suicide the truest art,
though life seemed hardly worth the trouble to discard.
The German colonels strolled the Île de la Cité—

some to the Louvre, some to the Place Pigalle.
"The loneliness of poets has been erased," cried Éluard,
in praise of Stalin. "Burn all the books," said dying Hugo Ball.
There is always a skeleton on the buffet.
I came. I sat down. I went away.

THE LITANY

This is a litany of lost things,
a canon of possessions dispossessed,
a photograph, an old address, a key.
It is a list of words to memorize
or to forget—of *amo, amas, amat,*
the conjugations of a dead tongue
in which the final sentence has been spoken.

This is the liturgy of rain,
falling on mountain, field, and ocean—
indifferent, anonymous, complete—
of water infinitesimally slow,
sifting through rock, pooling in darkness,
gathering in springs, then rising without our agency,
only to dissolve in mist or cloud or dew.

This is a prayer to unbelief,
to candles guttering and darkness undivided,
to incense drifting into emptiness.
It is the smile of a stone Madonna
and the silent fury of the consecrated wine,
a benediction on the death of a young god,
brave and beautiful, rotting on a tree.

This is a litany to earth and ashes,
to the dust of roads and vacant rooms,
to the fine silt circling in a shaft of sun,
settling indifferently on books and beds.
This is a prayer to praise what we become,
"Dust thou art, to dust thou shalt return."
Savor its taste—the bitterness of earth and ashes.

This is a prayer, inchoate and unfinished,
for you, my love, my loss, my lesion,
a rosary of words to count out time's
illusions, all the minutes, hours, days
the calendar compounds as if the past
existed somewhere—like an inheritance
still waiting to be claimed.

Until at last it is our litany, *mon vieux,*
my reader, my voyeur, as if the mist
steaming from the gorge, this pure paradox,
the shattered river rising as it falls—
splintering the light, swirling it skyward,
neither transparent nor opaque but luminous,
even as it vanishes—were not our life.

· II ·

I have heard the summer dust crying to be born.

—ROBINSON JEFFERS

ENTRANCE

Whoever you are: step out of doors tonight,
Out of the room that lets you feel secure.
Infinity is open to your sight.
Whoever you are.
With eyes that have forgotten how to see
From viewing things already too well-known,
Lift up into the dark a huge, black tree
And put it in the heavens: tall, alone.
And you have made the world and all you see.
It ripens like the words still in your mouth.
And when at last you comprehend its truth,
Then close your eyes and gently set it free.

(After Rilke)

NEW YEAR'S

Let other mornings honor the miraculous.
Eternity has festivals enough.
This is the feast of our mortality,
The most mundane and human holiday.

On other days we misinterpret time,
Pretending that we live the present moment.
But can this blur, this smudgy in-between,
This tiny fissure where the future drips

Into the past, this flyspeck we call *now*
Be our true habitat? The present is
The leaky palm of water that we skim
From the swift, silent river slipping by.

The new year always brings us what we want
Simply by bringing us along—to see
A calendar with every day uncrossed,
A field of snow without a single footprint.

METAMORPHOSIS

There were a few, the old ones promised us,
Who could escape. A few who once, when trapped
At the extremes of violence, reached out
Beyond the rapist's hand or sudden blade.

Their fingers branched and blossomed. Or they leapt
Unthinking from the heavy earth to fly
With voices—ever softer—that became
The admonitions of the nightingale.
They proved, like cornered Daphne twisting free,
There were a few whom even the great gods
Could not destroy.

          And you, my gentle ghost,
Did you break free before the cold hand clutched?
Did you escape into the lucid air
Or burrow secretly among the dark
Expectant roots, to rise again with them
As the unknown companion of our spring?

I'll never know, my changeling, where you've gone,
And so I'll praise you—flower, bird, and tree—
My nightingale awake among the thorns,
My laurel tree that marks a god's defeat,
My blossom bending on the water's edge,
Forever lost within your inward gaze.

PENTECOST

after the death of our son

Neither the sorrows of afternoon, waiting in the silent house,
Nor the night no sleep relieves, when memory
Repeats its prosecution.

Nor the morning's ache for dream's illusion, nor any prayers
Improvised to an unknowable god
Can extinguish the flame.

We are not as we were. Death has been our pentecost,
And our innocence consumed by these implacable
Tongues of fire.

Comfort me with stones. Quench my thirst with sand.
I offer you this scarred and guilty hand
Until others mix our ashes.

AFTER A LINE BY CAVAFY

for the poet John Finlay, dead of AIDS

Return and take me, distant afternoon,
Return and take hold of me
When the blue lake is dry white stone,
And the earth reclaims its arch of green.
Remember and repeat some confidence we shared,
Drunk with the promise of our new acquaintance,
Walking on the shore arguing ideas
As only the young can argue—
Passionate, naïve, and nervous with excitement,
Like hands touching for the first time—
We who were neither lovers nor intimates
And never met again.

A CALIFORNIA REQUIEM

I walked among the equidistant graves
New planted in the irrigated lawn.
The square, trim headstones quietly declared
The impotence of grief against the sun.

There were no outward signs of human loss.
No granite angel wept beside the lane.
No bending willow broke the once-rough ground
Now graded to a geometric plane.

My blessed California, you are so wise.
You render death abstract, efficient, clean.
Your afterlife is only real estate,
And in his kingdom Death must stay unseen.

I would have left then. I had made my one
Obligatory visit to the dead.
But as I turned to go, I heard the voices,
Faint but insistent. This is what they said.

"Stay a moment longer, quiet stranger.
Your footsteps woke us from our lidded cells.
Now hear us whisper in the scorching wind,
Our single voice drawn from a thousand hells.

"We lived in places that we never knew.
We could not name the birds perched on our sill,
Or see the trees we cut down for our view.
What we possessed we always chose to kill.

"We claimed the earth but did not hear her claim,
And when we died, they laid us on her breast,

But she refuses us—until we earn
Forgiveness from the lives we dispossessed.

"We are so tiny now—light as the spores
That rotting clover sheds into the air,
Dry as old pods burnt open by the sun,
Barren as seeds unrooted anywhere.

"Forget your stylish verses, little poet—
So sadly beautiful, precise, and tame.
We are your people, though you would deny it.
Admit the justice of our primal claim.

"Become the voice of our forgotten places.
Teach us the names of what we have destroyed.
We are like shadows the bright noon erases,
Weightlessly shrinking, bleached into the void.

"We offer you the landscape of your birth—
Exquisite and despoiled. We all share blame.
We cannot ask forgiveness of the earth
For killing what we cannot even name."

DESCENT TO THE UNDERWORLD

There is a famous cliff on Sparta's coast,
A headland covered by a thick-grown wood,
Where Cape Taenarus juts into the sea.
It's here the mouth of Hades opens up.
The high cliffs split apart, and a huge cave,
A gaping chasm, stretches its great jaws
And makes an entrance wide enough
For all mankind.

          At first the way is not
Entirely dark. Some daylight filters down
And gives the cave that same bleak iridescence
The sun shows in eclipse. But gradually
The path descends into unending twilight.
Your vision blurs, and only feeble streaks
Of rose and violet shimmer in the dark
Like the last fading embers of a sunset.

But then the pathway opens to a vast
And empty place, a hazy nothingness
That all humanity must come fill.
The journey now seems easy. The path itself
Begins to draw you down. Like waves that sweep
Whole fleets of ships unwillingly off course,
Wind pushes at your back. The dark turns ravenous,
And shadows stretch out from the walls to clutch—
They let no one return.

          Now at the bottom
The river Lethe runs as boundary,
Quiet and smooth, curving across the plain.
One drink will wash away the memory

Of all life's sorrow. To prevent the souls
From turning back to find the world of light,
The peaceful river twists and twists again
Just as the slow Maeander River does
In Phrygia, which bends back on itself
So many times that travelers scarcely know
Whether it seeks the seacoast or its source.

Beyond the Lethe, lies the foul Cocytus,
River of Tears, motionless as a swamp,
Where starving vultures and the sleepless owl
Shriek overhead their prophecies of pain.
Here in the branches of a tangled yew
Sits drowsy Sleep, while desperate Famine lies
Writhing on the ground, stretching her wasted jaws.
Here futile Shame averts his burning face—
Always too late—and thin Anxiety
Stalks nervously pursued by dark-eyed Fear.
Here is gnashing Pain and black-robed Sorrow,
Trembling Disease and iron-vested War,
And, last of all, Old Age, his staff in hand,
Tottering forward step by painful step.

There are no grassy meadows bright with flowers,
No fields of tasseled corn swaying in the wind,
No soft green vistas for the eye, or groves
Where branches bend with slowly sweetening fruit,
No breezes spiced with odors of the plum.
But only wasteland everywhere, the fields
Unwatered and untilled, the soil exhausted
And nothing moving on the silent land.

And this is how life ends—
This barren place, this country of despair,
Where no wind blows and darkness never lifts,
With hopeless sorrow twisting every shadow.
Dying is bitter, but eternity
Confined in this black place is worse.

(After Seneca)

THE END OF THE WORLD

"We're going," they said, "to the end of the world."
So they stopped the car where the river curled,
And we scrambled down beneath the bridge
On the gravel track of a narrow ridge.

We tramped for miles on a wooded walk
Where dog-hobble grew on its twisted stalk.
Then we stopped to rest on the pine-needle floor
While two ospreys watched from an oak by the shore.

We came to a bend, where the river grew wide
And green mountains rose on the opposite side.
My guides moved back. I stood alone,
As the current streaked over smooth flat stone.

Shelf by stone shelf the river fell.
The white water goosetailed with eddying swell.
Faster and louder the current dropped
Till it reached a cliff, and the trail stopped.

I stood at the edge where the mist ascended,
My journey done where the world ended.
I looked downstream. There was nothing but sky,
The sound of the water, and the water's reply.

· III ·

WORDS FOR MUSIC

Natives of poverty, children of malheur,
The gaiety of language is our seigneur.

—WALLACE STEVENS

SONG FOR THE END OF TIME

The hanged man laughs by the garden wall,
And the hands of the clock have stopped at the hour.
The cathedral angels are starting to fall,
And the bells ring themselves in the gothic tower.

Lock up your money and go bolt the door,
And don't dare look yourself in the eye.
Pray on your knees or cry on the floor
Or stare at the stars as they fall from the sky.

You may say that you're sorry for all that you've done,
You may swear on your honor and protest with tears,
But the moon is burning under the sun,
And nothing you do will stop what appears.

THE ARCHBISHOP

for a famous critic

O do not disturb the Archbishop,
Asleep in his ivory chair.
You must send all the workers away,
Though the church is in need of repair.

His Reverence is tired from preaching
To the halt, and the lame, and the blind.
Their spiritual needs are unsubtle,
Their notions of God unrefined.

The Lord washed the feet of His servants.
"The first shall be last," He advised.
The Archbishop's edition of Matthew
Has that troublesome passage revised.

The Archbishop declines to wear glasses,
So his sense of the world grows dim.
He thinks that the crowds at Masses
Have gathered in honor of him.

In the crypt of the limestone cathedral
A friar recopies St. Mark,
A nun serves stew to a novice,
A choirboy sobs in the dark.

While high in the chancery office
His Reverence studies the glass,
Wondering which of his vestments
Would look best at Palm Sunday Mass.

The saints in their weather-stained niches
Weep as the Vespers are read,
And the beggars sleep on the church steps,
And the orphans retire unfed.

On Easter the Lord is arisen
While the Archbishop breakfasts in bed,
And the humble shall find resurrection,
And the dead shall lie down with the dead.

THREE SONGS FROM *NOSFERATU*

1. ELLEN'S DREAM

I came to a table set for a feast,
Decked with silver and delicate lace.
The crystal shimmered in candlelight.
A long-stemmed rose adorned each place.
But the lace was torn and stained with rust,
The roses broken and bent askew.
The plates were empty. The room was cold,
And the only guest was you.

I heard the hush of a captured bird—
The twisted wings, the pounding heart.
I saw a fisherman take a knife
And carve his gleaming catch apart.
I watched the spider weave its web.
It sparkled in the beaded dew.
But when the moth lay in its trap,
I saw the prey was you.

I came down a stair to a bolted door.
I touched the lock, and it fell away.
I found a vast and sunless room.
I wanted to leave but had to stay.
The room was a chapel lit by candles,
But the cross had been broken in two.
The priest held a chalice of blood in his hands,
And on the altar was—you.

2. NOSFERATU'S SERENADE

I am the image that darkens your glass,
The shadow that falls wherever you pass.
I am the dream you cannot forget,
The face you remember without having met.

I am the truth that must not be spoken,
The midnight vow that cannot be broken.
I am the bell that tolls out the hours.
I am the fire that warms and devours.

I am the hunger that you have denied,
The ache of desire piercing your side.
I am the sin you have never confessed,
The forbidden hand caressing your breast.

You've heard me inside you speak in your dreams,
Sigh in the ocean, whisper in streams.
I am the future you crave and you fear.
You know what I bring. Now I am here.

3. MAD SONG

I sailed a ship
In the storm-wracked sea,
And all were drowned
Except for me.
I swam all night
Through death-cold waves
Till my shipmates called
From their sunken graves,
A lucky life for you, lad, a lucky life for you!

I fought through wars
In a barren land
Till none were left
Of my rugged band.
On a field of dead
Only I stood free.
Then a blind crow laughed
From a blasted tree,
A lucky life for you, lad, a lucky life for you!

I scaled a mountain
Of cold sharp stone.
The others fell,
And I climbed alone.
When I reached the top,
The winds were wild,
But a skull at my feet
Looked up and smiled,
A lucky life for you, lad, a lucky life for you!

BORROWED TUNES

1. ALLEY CAT LOVE SONG

Come into the garden, Fred,
For the neighborhood tabby is gone.
Come into the garden, Fred.
I have nothing but my flea collar on,
And the scent of catnip has gone to my head.
I'll wait by the screen door till dawn.

The fireflies court in the sweetgum tree.
The nightjar calls from the pine,
And she seems to say in her rhapsody,
"Oh, mustard-brown Fred, be mine!"
The full moon lights my whiskers afire,
And the fur goes erect on my spine.

I hear the frogs in the muddy lake
Croaking from shore to shore.
They've one swift season to soothe their ache.
In autumn they sing no more.
So ignore me now, and you'll hear my meow
As I scratch all night at the door.

2. THE BEGGAR'S NIGHTMARE

If wishes were horses, all beggars would ride
And gallop like squires through the green countryside,
But with nowhere to go, and no end in sight,
Still strapped to their stallions late in the night,
Jumping the hedge in the thick-grown park
As if demons pursued in the owl-haunted dark,
They will curse their fortunes with each hoofbeat
And beg to be beggars back on the street.

AT THE WATERFRONT CAFÉ

Docked beside the quiet river, yachts are rocking in the sun
While their skippers stop for cocktails to replay the race they've run.
Military in their khakis, they invade the chic café.
Smirnoff tinkles in their tumblers. No one's drinking Perrier.

    In the parking lot a valet
    Sunbathes by a sleek Mercedes
    Till he's prodded by a matron
    For directions to the Ladies'.

Meanwhile at a dockside table, virginal in tennis whites,
Figuring the least caloric way to staunch their appetites,
Sit two sweaty Junior Leaguers, wilting from their one-on-one.
Stoically they choose the fruitcup and a glass of Haut-Brion.

    Meanwhile like great diplomats
    With elegance and statesmanship,
    From the ruins of a luncheon
    Waiters excavate their tip.

Fair as Venus on a half shell, flanked by two aerobic beaus,
Shines a local sun-kissed princess, lambent in her jogging clothes.
When she smiles at the busboy, he starts grinning ear to ear.
Till she counters with a fleeting but still devastating sneer.

    At the upstairs bar a couple,
    Amorous despite the heat,
    Gropes in a manner more becoming
    To an Oldsmobile's back seat.

Now and then a ripple splashes from a power cruiser's wake
Or the shadow of a catfish flickers through the green opaque
Till the river reassembles like a placid mountain lake.
Then a doctor in a Piper swoops and makes the water shake.

    Waxed Bugatis, shiny Porsches
    Pour out from the parking lot
    While rococo clouds of dust
    Swirl above each emptied spot.

Wasted patrons head off homeward. Who knows which will not return?
Done in by a fatal face-lift or a tanning-parlor burn?
All their leveraged investments flattened by a market crash,
And their grandma's silver service pawned downtown for petty cash?

    But tonight I hope they prosper.
    Are they shallow? I don't care.
    Jealousy is all too common,
    Style and beauty much too rare.

CURRICULUM VITAE

The future shrinks
Whether the past
Is well or badly spent.

We shape our lives
Although their forms
Are never what we meant.

· IV ·

The gods have their own rules.

—OVID

JUNO PLOTS HER REVENGE

Thebes at night under the stars. The goddess speaks.

Call me sister of the thunder god.
That is the only title I have left.
Once I was wife and queen to Jupiter,
But now, abandoned by his love and shamed
By his perpetual adultery,
I leave my palace to his mistresses.
Why not choose earth when heaven is a whorehouse?

Even the Zodiac has now become
A pantheon of prostitutes and bastards.
Look at Callisto shining in the north,
That glittering slut now guides the Grecian fleet.
Or see how Taurus rises in the south,
Not only messenger of spring's warm nights
But the gross trophy of Europa's rape!
Or count the stormy Pleiades—those nymphs
Who terrorize the waves, once warmed Jove's bed.
Watch young Orion swaggering with his sword,
A vulgar upstart challenging the gods,
While gaudy Perseus flaunts his golden star.
Gape at the constellations Jove awarded
Castor and Pollux, his twin bastard sons.
And now not only Bacchus and his mother
Parade their ill-begotten rank in heaven,
But my husband, lord of lechery,
Discarding his last shred of decency,
Has crowned his drunken bastard's slut with stars!

But why rehearse long-standing grievances?
Tonight I have to face new aggravation—
From Thebes! This crude, depressing, backward land,

Less a nation than a vast bordello,
Full of ripe country girls eager to make me
Stepmother to my husband's indiscretions.
And now Alcmena will be deified
To occupy my place among the gods.
And Hercules, her son by Jupiter,
Is ready to assume his promised star.

I hate this Hercules. Even his begetting
Covered me with universal shame.
When Jupiter first coupled with Alcmena,
He cost the world a day, ordering Phoebus
To hold the rising chariots of the sun
Beneath the eastern waves—because one night
Was not enough to satisfy his lust.
I will not cool my anger in the waves,
But fuel it like a blacksmith's raging furnace
To forge a blade of merciless revenge.
My only peace will be eternal war.

But with what weapons? Every savage beast
Spawned by the blighted earth, every foul monster
Born in the angry sea or storm-tossed air,
Hercules has destroyed or overcome.
He leaves each battle freshened and renewed.
He takes the deadly labors I impose
And turns them to his credit. Pointlessly
My hate has made a hero out of him.
My anger proved the mother of his glory.
I fretted more in setting his twelve labors
Than that young braggart did in their completion.
Each time I sent him to his death, he smiled,
Always returning smugly with his trophies—

The lion's skin stretched out across his shield,
His arrowheads dipped in the Hydra's poison.

And now his conquests reach beyond the earth.
He batters down the gates of hell itself
And brings back spoils from the defeated depths.
I watched him come before the throne of Jove.
Yes, watched in horror, as he shamelessly
Displayed the sacred beast which he had seized
From Jove's own brother, having brushed aside
The guardians of hell as casually
As hands might wave aside a smudge of smoke.

What next? Why not bring Pluto bound in chains,
Enslave a deity equal to Jove
And occupy his throne to rule the dead?
Was it not blasphemous enough for Hercules
To trespass Hades, roving like a bandit,
Then break death's law returning to the light?
The door stands open to the afterlife,
The crowded shadows whisper of escape,
The solemn mysteries of death revealed.

But Hercules is proud of breaking laws.
He takes a boy's delight in boasting how
He meets my every challenge. He insults me,
Parading throughout Greece triumphantly,
Leading the sacred Cerberus to show
The terrifying mysteries of the grave
To every craning shopkeeper and schoolboy.
I watched the daylight shrink in fear. I saw
The blazing noon turn gray as the foul, black
Three-headed beast was circled by the crowd.

I watched the holy guardian of death,
Loaded with chains, gaped at like a sideshow,
And I was sick with shame that I, the queen
Of all the gods, had given the command.

But these are minor matters now—compared
With what I fear. Why wouldn't Hercules,
Who has subdued both earth and underworld,
Not try to conquer heaven next and seize
His father's office? Bacchus peacefully
Claimed his immortal place among the stars,
But Hercules knows nothing but brute force.
He will use violence to make his claim.
It will not bother such a man to rule
A decimated and demolished kingdom.

The time has come to turn my anger loose,
To set it like a pack of starving wolves
Howling after this ambitious brute—
To corner him, to rip him flesh from bone!
I will not delegate my huge revenge,
Nor will I use more monsters as my proxy.
No, even if the Titans were unchained,
Or the cold moon poured down its cruelest fiends,
I would not pit them all against this man.
But there is one sure way to conquer him.
I will make Hercules destroy himself.

So for the moment, let him forge ahead,
The arrogant fool, seeking his divinity,
So confident he is superior
To other men. Let him assume he's left
The underworld and all its ghosts behind.

For I will show him hell on earth! There is
A cavern buried deep in Tartarus
Where guilty souls are tortured through eternity
By unappeasable guardians of pain.
I summon up those primal deities.
Come to me, Discord, goddess of Destruction.
Bring up the secret horrors of the damned.
Come to me goddesses of Violence
And rash Impiety whose filthy hands
Are stained with family blood. Come to me, Error.
And come to me, you whom I most desire,
Goddess of Madness, who turns men on themselves,
You who will be the spur of my revenge.

Now, servants of the underworld, begin!
Let my voice shake the deepest pit of hell
And wake the Furies, daughters of the Night.
Come to me, sisters, with your hair aflame,
With savage claws. Inflict your punishments.
Revenge the desecration of the Styx.
Shatter his sanity. Make his soul burn
And make me mad as well, blinded by hate,
Senseless with anger, famished for his blood,
If it takes madness to conceive a plan
To break his mind and compel Hercules
To turn his strength to self-destructive fury.

The first act of my madness is a prayer—
For Hercules—"May he return home safe,
His strength intact, and find his little sons
Happy and healthy." Why resent his vigor?
I want him strong today. I want the same
Great force that conquered me to be his conqueror.

I crave occasion to applaud this hero,
Who triumphed over death's dominion,
As he begs for death and grovels for oblivion.

And, if I haven't always been a good
Stepmother to my husband's gifted son,
Today I'll make amends. I'll stand beside him
When frenzy blurs his sight, and help him send
Each arrow to its unsuspected mark.
I'll be his staunchest ally in the fight.
And when he finishes his giddy slaughter,
I'll have him raise his dripping hands to Jove
And ask for his admission into heaven!

I see the first bright tracings of the dawn.
The plan is set, and now I must be gone.

(After Seneca)

· V ·

O Many Named Beloved
Listen to my praise
Various as the seasons
Different as the days.

—SAMUEL MENASHE

CORNER TABLE

You tell me you are going to marry him.
You knew almost at once he was the one.
Your hands rest on the quilted tablecloth.
"Such clever hands," I used to say.
I gave them names I never spoke aloud.

You tell me how you met and where you'll live.
It's easier to watch your lips than listen.
Your eyes flash in the candlelight like knives.
The waiters drift by with their phantom meals.
Tonight the dead are dining with the dead.

You twist the wineglass slowly in your hand,
And I speak of other things. What matters most
Most often can't be said. Better to trust
The forms that hold our grief. We understand
This last mute touch that lingers is farewell.

LONG DISTANCE

Two weeks of silence broken by this call,
She holds the neutral phone against her cheek,
Hearing his whisper cross a continent.
Once words were never distant from his lips.
Now sound alone would stroke her like a kiss.

She still could tell him everything in touch
And read his certain answers in embrace.
But now his voice seems oddly out of place,
Almost anonymous, as if she overheard
A stranger talking on another line.

The conversation finished, phone in hand,
She wonders who has spoken, what was said?
Why is a lover's touch most keenly felt
The moment it is first withheld? She sees
The miles between them stretch beyond her reach.

She would forgive him now if he were here
And fall into his soothing arms like sleep.
His arms would be her answers, uninquired.
But words are never as precise as touch.
Now words that have no body ask her love.

MY DEAD LOVER

How miserable we were together, dear,
When we were young and wanted to be perfect.
You never condescended to be happy.
You wanted ecstasy—or nothing at all.

Your body was the first I ever knew
Better than my own. Your hands the first
I could surrender to. My dreams still search
The narrow room we used each afternoon.
We locked the door, but sun slipped through the blinds,
And time crept closer, always keeping count.

And now you are nowhere. You are nothing,
Not even ashes. How very like you, love,
To slip away again so skillfully.
You didn't even leave behind a grave
Where I might lay a wreath of old regrets
Beside your name, knowing you wouldn't care.
You hated scenes, especially good-byes.

The people walking past me on the pier
Know nothing of you. They are the ghosts.
I lift a hand of earth into the wind.
I offer it instead of ashes.
It isn't you the wind takes grain by grain.
You're free of earth, of time, even free of me.

Our rituals are never for the dead.

HOMAGE TO VALERIO MAGRELLI

I.

Tomorrow morning I will take a shower.
Nothing but that is certain.
A future of water and talc
in which nothing follows, and no one
knocks on the door. The crooked
river will fall through the steam, and I
will stand still like a hermit
in the lukewarm rain,
though no visions or temptations
will cross the clouded mirror.
Motionless and silent, traversed
by infinite streams,
I will stay in the current
like a tree trunk or a dead horse,
until I end, stranded in thought,
on the lonely delta of the spirit
as entangled as a woman's sex.

II.

I have finally learned
how to read the living
constellation of women
and men, to trace the lines
which connect them into figures.
And now I recognize the hints
which bind the disorder of the heavens.
Across this vault designed by thought
I discern light's revolution
and the wavering of signs.
So the day draws to a close
while I walk
in the silent garden of glances.

III.

I have often imagined that glances
survive the act of seeing
as if they were poles,
measuring rods, lances
thrown in a battle.
Then I think that in a room
one has just left
those same lines must stay behind
sometimes suspended there and crisscrossed
in the equilibrium of their design
untouched and overlaid like the wooden pieces
in a game of pick-up-sticks.

IV.

Especially in weeping
the soul reveals
its presence
and through secret pressure
changes sorrow into water.
The first budding of the spirit
is in the tear,
a slow and transparent word.
Then following this elemental alchemy
thought turns itself into substance
as real as a stone or an arm.
And there is nothing uneasy in the liquid
except the mineral
anguish of matter.

V.

And the crack in the teacup opens
A lane to the land of the dead.

—W. H. AUDEN

. . . as when a crack
crosses a cup.

—R. M. RILKE

I have from you this red
cup with which to drink to all my days
one by one
in the pale mornings, the pearls
of the long necklace of thirst.
And if it drops and breaks, I, too,
will be shattered, but compassionately
I will repair it
to continue the kisses uninterrupted.
And each time the handle
or the rim gets cracked
I will go back to glue it
until my love will have completed
the hard, slow work of a mosaic.

It comes down along the white
slope of the cup
along the concave interior
and flashes, just like lightning—

the crack,
black, permanent,
the sign of a storm
still thundering
over this resonant landscape
of enamel.

VI.

In the evening when the light is dim,
I hide in bed and collect
the silhouettes of reasoning
which silently run across my limbs.
It is here I must weave
the tapestry of thought
and arranging the threads of my self
design my own figure.
This is not work
but a kind of workmanship.
First out of paper, then from the body.
To provoke thought into form,
molded according to a measure.
I think of a tailor
who is his own fabric.

(After the Italian of Valerio Magrelli)

ACCOMPLICE

In dusty fields I harvested the vine
And sweated at the lever as the grapes were pressed.
My aching hands still clutched their vagrant wages,
Sleeping in the cold barracks of the dispossessed.

But now at dawn, beyond the reach of reason,
I wake in the chateau between your tangled sheets,
My sunburnt arm across your naked shoulder,
The mute accomplice of our mutual defeat.

THE BARGAIN

Nothing so sordid as an affair,
nor half so safe. How did we know
that night merely from a look
that friendship had become
more dangerous than lust?

I had forgotten the sharp
exactitude of touch, the fierce
articulation of a look
returned, the hungry thrill of pleasure
which cannot be prolonged.

For without a word we struck
our bargain—ignorant of its price,
dear beyond our means—thinking
that we could cultivate
the act we would deny.

Nothing so usual as lust,
nothing so common as a lie,
we tell ourselves—as we pursue
this exegesis of desire
more tangled than deceit.

SPIDER IN THE CORNER

Cold afternoon: rain spattering the windows,
the dampness spreading slowly like a mold
in the poverty of gray November light.

Another day of books and spoiled plans,
of cigarettes and sitting still
in rooms too small for us. How little there

is left to talk about except the weather.
And so we tolerate the silence
like the spider in the corner neither one

of us will kill. Yes, the doorway whispers.
But we will stay—until the weather clears,
the endless rain that keeps us here together.

FOR SALE

Your first home, your handyman's special!
Leading us through the dark wallpapered rooms,
you joked about the debt

confident that new fixtures, another coat of paint
would heal the ceiling cracks
and make the scuffed floors gleam.

Someone else's old bouquets
festooned the bedroom walls—bright
pink wallpaper rusting into brown.

Windmill upon windmill
floated in the delft-blue bathroom.
The paper curled at the corners.

Getting our coats, we saw the paint cans
unopened in the closet, your ladder
folded flat against the wall.

Standing on the porch, you waved
good-bye, good-bye, as if we were the ones
going on a journey.

TIME TRAVEL

Surely the comic books and movies have it right.
The past is waiting for us somewhere—
The table set, soup steaming on the stove.

No theme song, please, or special effects.
This ordinary room with its preposterous lamp
And blue-chintz sofa will suffice.

How long it took to recognize
The shameless modesty of our desire—
Only to possess what we already had.

Let me unlock the door and step inside.
Will you be there at the other end,
Waiting unawares—

There on the morning that we met?

SUMMER STORM

We stood on the rented patio
While the party went on inside.
You knew the groom from college.
I was a friend of the bride.

We hugged the brownstone wall behind us
To keep our dress clothes dry
And watched the sudden summer storm
Floodlit against the sky.

The rain was like a waterfall
Of brilliant beaded light,
Cool and silent as the stars
The storm hid from the night.

To my surprise, you took my arm—
A gesture you didn't explain—
And we spoke in whispers, as if we two
Might imitate the rain.

Then suddenly the storm receded
As swiftly as it came.
The doors behind us opened up.
The hostess called your name.

I watched you merge into the group,
Aloof and yet polite.
We didn't speak another word
Except to say good-night.

Why does that evening's memory
Return with this night's storm—

A party twenty years ago,
Its disappointments warm?

There are so many *might-have-beens,*
What-ifs that won't stay buried,
Other cities, other jobs,
Strangers we might have married.

And memory insists on pining
For places it never went,
As if life would be happier
Just by being different.

THE LOST GARDEN

If ever we see those gardens again,
The summer will be gone—at least our summer.
Some other mockingbird will concertize
Among the mulberries, and other vines
Will climb the high brick wall to disappear.

How many footpaths crossed the old estate—
The gracious acreage of a grander age—
So many trees to kiss or argue under,
And greenery enough for any mood.
What pleasure to be sad in such surroundings.

At least in retrospect. For even sorrow
Seems bearable when studied at a distance,
And if we speak of private suffering,
The pain becomes part of a well-turned tale
Describing someone else who shares our name.

Still, thinking of you, I sometimes play a game.
What if we had walked a different path one day,
Would some small incident have nudged us elsewhere
The way a pebble tossed into a brook
Might change the course a hundred miles downstream?

The trick is making memory a blessing,
To learn by loss the cool subtraction of desire,
Of wanting nothing more than what has been,
To know the past forever lost, yet seeing
Behind the wall a garden still in blossom.

UNSAID

So much of what we live goes on inside—
The diaries of grief, the tongue-tied aches
Of unacknowledged love are no less real
For having passed unsaid. What we conceal
Is always more than what we dare confide.
Think of the letters that we write our dead.

NOTES ON THE POEMS

Elegy with Surrealist Proverbs as Refrain

The two refrains are translated from Paul Éluard and Benjamin Peret's *152 Proverbes Mis au Goût du Jour* (*152 Proverbs Done for Today's Taste*) published in 1925. The French proverbs read, *"Il y a toujours un squelette dans le buffet"* and *"Je suis venu, je me suis assis, je suis parti."* All of the incidents and quotations in the poem are true.

After a Line by Cavafy

This poem plays with the opening lines of Constantine Cavafy's "Return." It borrows phrasing from both Rae Dalven's translation ("Return often and take me, / beloved sensation, return and take me") and Edmund Keeley and Philip Sherrard's version ("Come back often and take hold of me, / sensation that I love, come back and take hold of me").

Descent to the Underworld

This poem is freely adapted from Theseus' account of the underworld from Act III of Seneca's *Hercules Furens* (*The Madness of Hercules*). The translation suggests how Dante and Eliot were influenced by Seneca's description of Hell.

Words for Music

The "Three Songs from *Nosferatu*" were written for the composer Alva Henderson as part of an opera libretto based on F. W. Murnau's silent film.

Juno Plots Her Revenge

Juno is both the wife and sister to Jupiter. Hercules is the illegitimate son of Jupiter with the mortal woman Alcmena. Juno's rant is the opening speech of Seneca's *Hercules Furens*. As Juno's soliloquy begins, Hercules has completed the last of his twelve labors, and Jupiter is considering deifying him.

This book was based on a design by Tree Swenson.
It is set in Galliard type by Stanton Publication Services, Inc.,
and manufactured by Thomson-Shore on acid-free paper.